D1378401

EXPLORE THE U.S.A.

INDIANA

Anita Yasuda

AV²
BY WEIGL™
LET'S READ
ADDED VALUE · AUDIO VISUAL

www.av2books.com

LET'S READ

AV²
BY WEIGL™

ADDED VALUE • AUDIO VISUAL

Go to **www.av2books.com,**
and enter this book's
unique code.

BOOK CODE

C 8 7 3 4 0 8

AV² by Weigl brings you media
enhanced books that support
active learning.

AV² provides enriched content that supplements and complements this book. Weigl's AV² books strive to create inspired learning and engage young minds in a total learning experience.

Your AV² Media Enhanced books come alive with...

Audio
Listen to sections of
the book read aloud.

Video
Watch informative
video clips.

Embedded Weblinks
Gain additional information
for research.

Try This!
Complete activities and
hands-on experiments.

Key Words
Study vocabulary, and
complete a matching
word activity.

Quizzes
Test your knowledge.

Slide Show
View images and
captions, and prepare
a presentation.

... and much, much more!

Published by AV² by Weigl
350 5th Avenue, 59th Floor
New York, NY 10118
Website: www.av2books.com   www.weigl.com

Library of Congress Cataloging-in-Publication Data

Yasuda, Anita.
 Indiana / Anita Yasuda.
   p. cm. -- (Explore the U.S.A.)
 Includes bibliographical references and index.
 ISBN 978-1-61913-347-1 (hard cover : alk. paper)
 1. Indiana--Juvenile literature. I. Title.
 F526.3.Y37 2012
 977.2--dc23
                          2012015071

Printed in the United States of America in North Mankato, Minnesota
1 2 3 4 5 6 7 8 9   16 15 14 13 12

052012
WEP040512

Project Coordinator: Karen Durrie
Art Director: Terry Paulhus

Weigl acknowledges Getty Images as the primary image supplier
for this title.

INDIANA

Contents

3

This is Indiana.
It is called the Hoosier State.
A person from Indiana is called
a Hoosier.

This is the shape of Indiana. It is in the middle part of the United States. Indiana is bordered by four states.

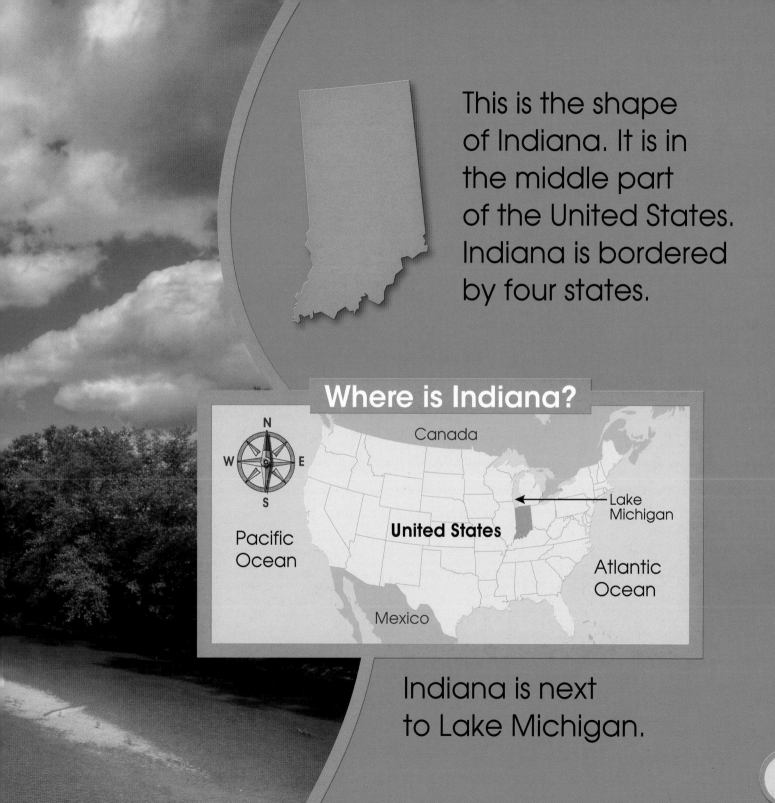

Where is Indiana?

Canada

N
W   E
S

Pacific Ocean

United States

Lake Michigan

Atlantic Ocean

Mexico

Indiana is next to Lake Michigan.

Wilbur Wright was born
on a farm in Indiana.
Wilbur and his brother Orville
wanted to fly. They made
the first working airplane.

The Wright brothers made
many kites and gliders
before making airplanes.

The peony is the state flower of Indiana. Peony bushes can live for more than 100 years.

The Indiana state seal has a man and an American bison.

The man on the seal is a woodsman with an ax.

This is the state flag
of Indiana. It is blue
and yellow. It has
a gold torch and stars.

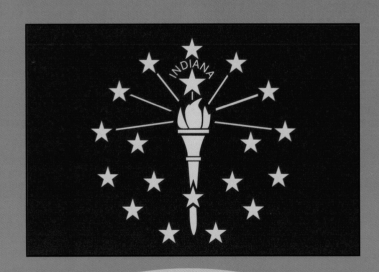

There are 19 stars
because Indiana is
the 19th state.

13

The state bird of Indiana is the cardinal. The female is brown, and the male is red. Cardinals make nests from twigs and vines.

The cardinal is the state bird for seven states.

This is the largest city in Indiana. It is named Indianapolis. It is the state capital.

The Indianapolis 500 car race is held in Indianapolis.

Indiana has limestone.
Indiana limestone is used
all over the world. Limestone
takes millions of years to form.

The Empire State
Building is made of
Indiana limestone.

19

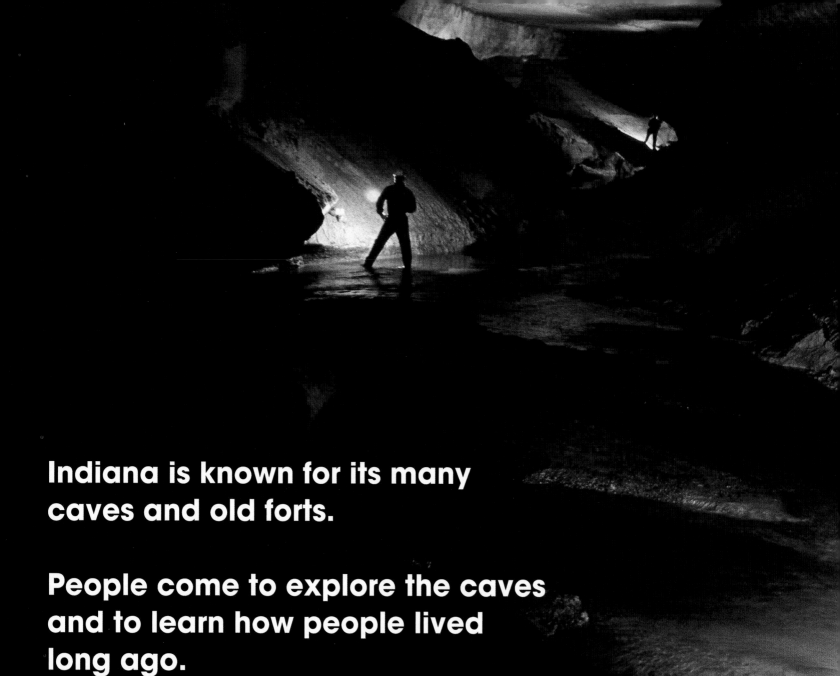

Indiana is known for its many
caves and old forts.

People come to explore the caves
and to learn how people lived
long ago.

INDIANA FACTS

These pages provide detailed information that expands on the interesting facts found in the book. These pages are intended to be used by adults as a learning support to help young readers round out their knowledge of each state in the *Explore the U.S.A.* series.

Pages 4–5

Indiana is well known by its nickname, the Hoosier State. Hoosier is one of the oldest of the state's nicknames. By the 1830s, the nickname was being widely used, but it is not known where the name Hoosier comes from. The name *Indiana* means "land of the Indians." This is a reference to the many American Indians that once lived in the region.

Pages 6–7

On December 11, 1816, Indiana joined the United States as the 19th state. Indiana is the smallest of all midwestern states. It is bordered by Michigan to the north, Ohio to the east, Illinois to the west, and Kentucky to the south. Indiana's state motto is "The Crossroads of America" because of its central location. Fourteen interstate highways run through Indiana.

Pages 8–9

Wilbur Wright was born on April 16, 1867, in Millville, Indiana. From a young age, he was interested in flight. With his brother Orville, he built the first successful airplane. The first flight took place on December 17, 1903, in Kitty Hawk, North Carolina.

Pages 10–11

The peony became the official state flower in 1957. The peony blooms in the late spring. Indiana's state seal shows a pioneer scene. There is a woodsman with his ax and a buffalo jumping over a log. The Sun is setting behind hills in the background.

A state flag design contest was held during Indiana's 1916 centennial celebration. In 1917, the winning design by Paul Hadley became the official state flag. The 19 stars on the flag symbolize Indiana's position as the 19th state to join the United States. The flag's yellow torch represents liberty and enlightenment. The large star above the torch represents Indiana.

Male and female cardinals build nests in the spring using twigs, vines, and other plant materials. The female cardinal lays two to five eggs. She keeps the eggs warm while the male cardinal protects the nest. Males may attack intruders. They may see their reflections in a window and fly at it, believing they are seeing another cardinal.

Indianapolis became the state capital in 1820. Today, a network of highways runs through the city. More than 800,000 people live in Indianapolis. The city is home to the famous Indianapolis 500. This is a 500-mile (804-km), 200-lap auto race that is held every Memorial Day weekend.

Millions of years ago, Indiana was a shallow ocean bed. Limestone is a rock formed from marine fossils. Some of the biggest limestone deposits are found in Indiana. About 2.7 million cubic feet (76,400 cubic meters) of limestone are taken from Indiana quarries each year. There are hundreds of limestone caves in Indiana, including Wyandotte, Marengo, and Bluespring Caverns.

Visitors come to Indiana to enjoy nature and see historic sites such as Fort Wayne, which was built near the site of a Miami Indian village. They also come to explore the limestone caves and underground caverns. Bluespring Caverns can be seen from a tour boat that travels more than 1 mile (1.6 kilometers) on an underground river.

KEY WORDS

Research has shown that as much as 65 percent of all written material published in English is made up of 300 words. These 300 words cannot be taught using pictures or learned by sounding them out. They must be recognized by sight. This book contains 55 common sight words to help young readers improve their reading fluency and comprehension. This book also teaches young readers several important content words, such as proper nouns. These words are paired with pictures to aid in learning and improve understanding.

Page	Sight Words First Appearance
4	a, from, is, it, state, the, this
7	by, four, in, next, of, part, to, where
8	and, before, farm, first, his, made, many, on, they, was
11	American, an, can, has, live, for, man, more, than, with, years
12	are, because, there
15	all, makes, long
16	car, city, named
19	over, takes, used, world
20	come, how, its, learn, old, people

Page	Content Words First Appearance
4	Indiana, Hoosier, person
7	Lake Michigan, shape, United States
8	airplane, brother, gliders, kites, Wilbur Wright
11	ax, bison, bushes, flower, peony, seal, woodsman
12	flag, stars, torch
15	bird, cardinal, female, male, nests, twigs, vines
16	capital, Indianapolis, race
19	Empire State Building, limestone, millions
20	caves, forts

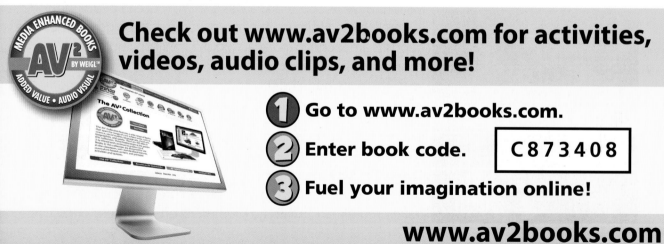